A book of poems
A collection of love poems
by
Jessika Crump

Jessika Crump,
　　　The Poetry of My Life | Poetry

Desert Spirits Publishing

ISBN-13: 978-0615827636
ISBN-10: 0615827632

The Poetry of My Life
A Collection of Poetry

by Jessika Crump

Desert Spirits Publishing

Table of Contents

Table of Content

The Poetry of My Life

LOVE
I've written many love poems over experiences, feelings, or watching someone else go through a tough time.

Break it off
Break all of this off
Break off all of the secrets
Break off everything that you're hiding
Break off these emotional feelings
Break off whatever is happening everyday
Break off every single feeling I have towards you
Break off every single feeling you have towards me
Break off us
Break off everything
Break off this love
Break off the 'hello's'
Break off the goodbye's

Can't
I can't do this anymore
You are everywhere I look
No matter where I am
You are there
I'm freaking out
Please make it stop
Forgive me
Take me back
I can't take it anymore
I'm sorry
I miss you
Please forgive me
I am very sorry

Jessika Crump

Fixing
This feeling is confusing
This feeling makes me sad
Can you make it clearer for me
Can you clarify the situation for me
Once you do, make it better please
Right now it stinks
This isn't what I had in mind
I want happiness, love, and comfort
I have sadness, despair, and discomfort
Help this
Help me
Can it get better for me
Can anything get better for me
Am I blind
Can I not see
Apparently, because I can't see your way

Continued

Where's the love
What about the happiness
Have they died
Have they left and will never return
Please answer
Give me comfort
Give me love
Give me happiness
Please provide these things for me
Let me see the errors
Let me fix my errors
Fix this
Fix me
Help me seek the things I need
Right now, you are no help
You just stand back and watch me
Just like a statue, like life

Love's a word
What is love but a mere word
What is love but a mere action
How can you love if no one love's you too
Love, what's the definition
Love is an intense feeling of deep affection
How do you know love when it's there
How do you know love when it's gone
Love can be anywhere
Love can be nowhere
Love, it's just a mere word

Me and you
Me and you would be if you wanted us to
Me and you could be great together
We both have so much in common that you don't see
You can't see how much we are alike
Me and you are compatible
We would be together is you wanted us to like I do
I know you might not want this
But it sure would be great
If you have ever thought about us being together,
That thought would last me a lifetime

My darling
This is a tribute to him
Who is loving, kind, and shy to everyone
Who always smiles, laughs, and shines towards people
Who never argues, insults, and contradicts anyone
Who taught me to open up, love again, and lose again
Who helped me to learn, laugh, and express
This is a tribute to him
This is a tribute to my lost love

The edge
At the edge of my open wound
I saw it glow, slowly starting to close itself
Half my wound stayed open while the rest healed
The top of my wound
Scarred me for life and forever
Half had closed but is able to open again whenever it pleases

This song, Love song
This song is a love song
This song is our love song
We don't know what they are saying
We don't know how to explain what they are saying
They are speaking a different language
They are making love sound foreign to our minds
This is our love song
This is our love life
We don't want to tell anyone
We don't want it to get out at all
They would break apart
They wouldn't understand
This wouldn't make sense to others
This wouldn't be enough for some people
We can't tell anyone

Us
What is this
What can it be
Can it be that way
Can it be better
Fix us
Fix this
Please, I know how you feel
I feel it too
Of course I do
How could I not
You are amazing
You are the air to my lungs
You are the blood in my veins
The brain in my head
The sun to my dark days
The comfort in my life
You are a part of me
Please, fix this problem
Fix us
Fix this

continued

It's not a break, it's not a break up
Cause we never started
I wish we would have started
I wish we would not be awkward together
I'm wishing we could still hug
I'm wishing we could be how we use to be
Like the old days
I wish you would look lovingly at me
I wish you could still cheer me up
I'm wishing you were up to it
I'm wishing we could change
I wish we could go away
And start anew
I know you want to
I want us together too
Because I love you

Valentine's Day
Victory lost forever
Anyone out there
Last like always
Eventually will be found
Negative attitude
Tormenting relationships
Irritating people
Nothing anywhere
Empty soul
Sucks
Day to myself
Alone again
Yourself is waiting for chocolate

What do I do
What should I do about this
This issue is an insane issue
I can't handle all of this work
This is to trippy for me to handle it all
I don't know if I can do this
What if I can't do this
Would you help me get back up on my feet and to stand tall
If I trip and fall and scrape my knee would you help me
What do I do
What do I do if you aren't there for me
What will I end up doing without you
You need to be here with me
For me
What do I do
What should I do

You and me
You and me should be together
We are perfect when we are,
Or so I thought
When you aren't here,
I hate it
I'm so lonely without you
This shouldn't happen
I made the wrong choice
The wrong decision
I'm oh so sorry
Please forgive me
This is horrible
I'm terrified
If you won't help me
Who will

You are
You are my everything
You are the light to my day
You are the stars to my night sky
You are the fat boy to my cake
You are my everything
Why do you have to be everything
Why can't you see this happening
Why are you so oblivious to this all
Why do you have to deny it like it's not there
Why can't you except this
Why can't you just let this all seep in
Why can't you just let this happen like it should
Why do you have to be everything

You can always
You always can make my day when I'm down in the dumps
When you hug me, I just want to melt in your arms
If I see you and you smile at me my eyes almost melt inside
I love everything you do for me and love why you do it
You can, no matter what, always make me happy
You always make me smile no matter what
If I am already happy you make me happier
I can't hold what I feel inside when I'm with you
You make me blush even if you just smile and wave hi
I love the way you make me feel when I'm around you
You make me feel loved

You
You are bitter, mean and harmful
You can't always be right
Get use to it
You are not perfect, no one is
But of course you think you are
Seriously, you are over conceded
You think you are on top of the world
But you aren't
Not even close
This is the real you
And it's very sad to see it
I shed tears for you
You may have outer beauty
But no inner beauty
None at all, cause you're selfish
Don't be this way
I bet you could do better
Even be better
You still have a couple years ahead of you
So use them

Continued

You can change your ways you can change your path
Try it, because you may like it
I know you can improve
But right now, I don't like you
Not one bit
Do better
Be better
Try your hardest
If you have friends, let them help
For once in your life be nice
Be pure
You can change
But it's your decision
Your move
Just make it

You're leaving
You're leaving, leaving me
All alone and I don't know why
All I see is black
No clouds in the skies
You're leaving, leaving me
Who ever told you that you have to go
They were wrong
They don't love you like I do
I see you day after day
But now I see gray
It's getting clear
I see now why you leave
You are scared
Scared of what will happen if you stay
I am with you and I'll never leave

Random

I wrote some random poems just to be funny or if I didn't have enough emotional inspiration to write a serious one.

The baby
The baby is crying
It won't stop, it won't eat, and it won't sleep
My ears want to go flying away
The baby just needs to count sheep and sleep
If only the baby could count
It would go to sleep and things would be okay
He cries in such a big amount at a time
My ears almost want to run away
Please make this baby stop
It's driving me crazy
Before my ears go pop
I think things are going hazy

Chocolate milk
Milk is good for your health
But chocolate milk is good for your taste buds health
Milk is white
Chocolate milk is brown
Regular milk comes out of white cows
Chocolate milk comes from brown cows
Milk is awesome
Chocolate milk is fantastic

Hello
Hello there
I do indeed have a name
I do indeed have a face
I am indeed a person
Hello to you
You are a person
You definitely have a name
You most likely have a face
Hello my fellow person

I am blue
I am a closed in, suffocating heart
I am the ocean with calm water and big creatures
I am the tears you are scared to shed upon your face

Mellifluous Unicorns
This subject might be risible
But the unicorn finding is a serious matter
Tracking down unicorns is frustraneous
They think we are their nemesis
And that is luculent
But we are friendly
Even the ones who are languorous
Unicorns are very mellifluous
When they are scared they turn diaphanous
Really old unicorns are very frangible
But most young unicorns are callipygian
Don't worry, these unicorns won't spread any miasma
There has been only one person to find a unicorn
This person said it was zaftig and had a winsome personality
He tried to get a picture with quiescence but it vanished
From then on, no one has ever caught sight of a unicorn
Until now

Movies
Movies are moving pictures that can amuse us for a little while
Movies can make someone forget the bad day they've been
having
Movies can take our minds off of mostly anything
Movies are great inventions that has made so many people
famous
Movies make us get false hope, which isn't always the best but
oh well
Movies give us a get-a-way from life for a little bit, until we
come back
Movies are fantastic

My day
My day has gone okay
I could be better
I just wanna eat better today
I don't know how much longer I can go without eating
I haven't eaten breakfast or lunch at all
I really want some lunch
There is nothing to eat
There is nowhere to go
I just want some food then everything will be one with the
world

Permit
Might go get my permit tomorrow
So scared I won't pass my first time
Waiting for the right chance to go
Studying so I pass it
Nervous to know what will happen to me
Excited to be able to finally drive on the road
What will I get
What will happen
So many questions to be answered
So many problems to be solved

Poems
I have to write only two more things
I can't write anymore journals
I might explode if I do
I have to write poems
I have nothing to say in a journal, there's nothing to say
I can't say blah-blah-blah the entire page
I can't just write a fake journal, that's cheating
I would still have nothing to say
I have to write a poem
I have nothing to say

Scream
Scream as loud as you can
No one can hear you
No one will listen
Hold it inside
It's useless
You can try and scream as loud as you can
No one will hear you
No one will listen
Screaming is a useless privilege
You could scream when you're excited, sad, or scared
Again, no one cares
No one will listen or hear you
No one cares if you scream your head off for any reason
They don't actually care
So scream
No one hears you
No one listens

Testing
So many signs on the road
So many rules for the road
There's DUI's
There's motorcycle rules
Are the rules ever going to end
Are the questions going to be easy or not
If not, help me
I need to study
I need to practice
I have to pass
Wish me luck

Them
They are animals
They are dogs
They give you the eyes when they want something
They will growl if they don't get it
They will play until they get bored then leave
They are hungry all the time
Like a puppy, they can't control what they do, ever
They constantly need attention
They are happy to get in a fight when it's needed
They are boys

This is who
This is who
This is me
This is you
This is us
What are you doing here
What am I doing here
What are they doing over there
Nothing
No one is doing anything anywhere
What's going on
Nothing
How's your day going
It's going
This is who
This is me
This is you
This is us
THIS IS EVERYONE

This poem
This is a poem
It doesn't have a rhyme scheme
It doesn't express anything
It is a poem
This is a poem
Is it going good
There is nothing to say here
There is nothing to do anywhere
This is a poem
I am writing a poem in a room
You are reading this poem in a place
I am saving this poem
This is a poem

What if things happened
What if you could press your temple and it played music
inside you
I would never use headphones
I would listen to music constantly
What is we loved and never lost
I would love him and only him forever
What if the world ended
I would go peacefully and lovingly
What if all you could do was think
I would think about life, love, and laughter

School
I wrote some poems about school because it was on my mind
for awhile and I had to get it off my chest.

Grades

My grades are important
They need to be my entire world
You can't be in the middle of us
I need to be able to keep them up
No matter what they need to be amazing
My parents aren't expecting all A's and B's
But they need to be C's or higher
You can't ruin that
You can't go and ruin all my hard work that I've done
Back up and leave us alone
Leave me and my grades alone
Let us be so we can work alone
Be behind us, following, so we are alone
Me and my grades need to work together for once
I need to keep my grades happy by being high

MORP day
MORP went good I guess
He didn't know how to dance
I had to teach him how to
Other than that it was a good time
Dinner was so much fun
We laughed a lot
We all had a great time
It didn't go perfectly
But it got pretty close to it
Fun times on Friday night

My paper
I know I waited tell the last minute
But I didn't want to finish it
I want to finish it now
But I don't know how
What if I can't finish everything on time
What would the world bring
I can't really pay attention
I have so much tension
There is too much noise
There are too many toys
There are too many kids
Why can't their mouths be covered with lids

Regional's
Our competition was yesterday
Hearts raced and blood was pumping
Got on the floor and did awesome
Looked at our score when it got posted
We got 12th out of 18
But got the 1st inn our division
Didn't make it to finals, was a little upset
But drumline made it
I was so proud of them
We all had a great time
We all made good memories

School
School is very important in anyone's life
School should not be wasted for something else not important
School should be taken seriously, not as a joke
School is a subject in life
School is a course in life that has to be taken
If school is not taken, it comes back to bite you in the butt
Take school, learn in school, and focus on school when
necessary
School is very important in everyone's life

Tomorrow
Tomorrow is the first day of the fourth quarter
Tomorrow is a new day of a new age
Tomorrow is like a fresh start
Tomorrow is going to be a fun day, at least I hope
Tomorrow is tomorrow
Tomorrow is school
Tomorrow is also a doctor's appointment, oh yay
Tomorrow is Tuesday
I am excited for tomorrow

Inspirational
I write inspirational quotes to try and help people along the
best I can in my own words.

Done
I am finished with all these people
I am finished with all this trash talk
I just want all of this to be over
Why can't it all just disappear
All of it should go to a different universe
Just leave, let me be
Why can't you all just leave me at peace
Why can't it all just let me be
This is all so irritating
I am done with everyone
I am done with everything
This is idiotic
Good day, please be on your way

Glasses

Glasses are seeing goggles for the eyes
They are things to help us see everything
They can help us see love, help us see traffic, help us see
people
Glasses can help us with everything
They can help us even if we don't want the help
They can help us even if we don't use them
Glasses are angles for the eyes
They are help for life
They are glasses for life

I don't know
No one really knows anything
I don't really know anything
You don't really know anything
No one really understands everything
You don't really understand anything
I don't really understand anything
Think about everything you know,
Do you really know that
Does your teacher really know that
No one really knows anything besides the universe
They are called guesses and hypothesizes for a reason
No one really knows or understands anything in life
Not even life itself
No one will ever understand life itself or what we were made to
do
No one knows anything
We don't know anything
I don't know anything
You don't know anything

Life

Life can always be positive and on the bright side
Life is a gift that we are given to have fun in
Some people are not responsible with the gift and waist it
Some others can't handle the gift so give it up
Other's know how to handle and use it but use it wisely
Life is here to have fun and make some mistakes
Then it gives you the chance to fix your mistakes
And gives you a 2nd chance to try again
Not everyone knows they have a 2nd chance
Don't give up the gift because they can't handle it
Don't give up life because you can't handle

Mix up
"This morning I cut my arm off" (Aron Ralston)
"The day you die" (American Beauty)
"The horror. The horror" (Apocalypse Now)
"I said I want the truth" (Chinatown)
"Every man dies, not every man really lives" (Braveheart)
"Who's the target audience… People with eyes" (Argo)
"I'm an agent of chaos. Oh, and you know the thing about chaos? It's fair!" (Dark Knight)
"Survival is the spirit. The soul, my soul is as ready as is my body. Fear is why you fail" (The Dark Knight Rises)
"You will be investigating thieves, misers, bully's, the most detestable collection of people you will ever meet." (The Girl with the Dragon Tattoo)

My dream
In my dream, I was a question
I was trying to find a hero
Trying to find an answer
I felt sadness
I felt alone
I never found him
I never found it
I crouched in the cement by myself
I was alone and upset
I wanted my hero
My answer
I wanted my answer
My man
But it wouldn't show
He wouldn't show
I waited, but nothing
No one, nothing showed
I cried out of pain, grasping my pounding head

Story of 9/11
9/11 ruined many people's lives
They lost close friends and family
"A sad soul can kill quicker then a germ." And most know it's
true (John Steinbeck)
Who could love again if you lost someone so close to you?
Some still morn in agony almost everyday
"I am convinced that material things can contribute a lot to
Making one's life pleasant, but, basically, if you do not have
Very good friends and relatives who matter to you, life will
Be really empty and sad and material things cease to be
Important." (David Rockefeller)
So many people worked there, and so many lives were lost
"It is sad not to love, but it is much sadder not to be able to
love." (Miguel de Unamuno)

Jessika Crump

Think
Let me ask you some questions
How do you feel
Do single people wear couple rings
Do babies steel
Can you play with fire,
And not get burnt
Can you drive a car with a missing tire
In shade, can you still get burnt
Can someone innocent do a bad thing
Are you thinking?
Can a lemon on a closed wound sting
Are you thinking about how your being, seeing, and feeling
Good
I want you to think
The answer to the questions not directed to you are
YES
Don't let your steam be covered by your hood

To say
You always need to realize
How a person feels inside
How you feel in your heart is your own personality
You never know how they feel
Unless you can step in their shoes
They might
Be sad or depressed even
So try to make them see the bright side
Whoever said life would be easy
I say that they are wrong
No matter what you do
It's still all up to you
Your life is up to no one else
But yourself

What
What do I do?
With this or with that?
What do I do with my life?
Can anyone answer my big question?
Probably not
But that's okay
I will figure it out eventually
I can't make a decision without hurting someone
So how do I decide on what to do with this?
I don't decide
I just have to let it work itself out
But for how long?
Tell whenever it solves itself I guess
It will eventually happen no matter what, right?
I will have to hurt someone in order to choose
But it will work itself out
It will be okay, I hope anyway

Who am I
Who am I
Am I me
Am I actually ever me
No, I act like someone else
Who am I
Am I me
Can I ever be just me
Why can I not be me
Why do I have to act like someone else
Who am I
I'm scared, frightened even
I don't want to be the real me
What if people don't like the true me
Who am I
I am no one

www.ingramcontent.com/pod-product-compliance
Lightning Source LLC
Chambersburg PA
CBHW031333040426
42443CB00005B/321